OPTICAL ILLUSIONS

A TRICK OF THE LIGHT

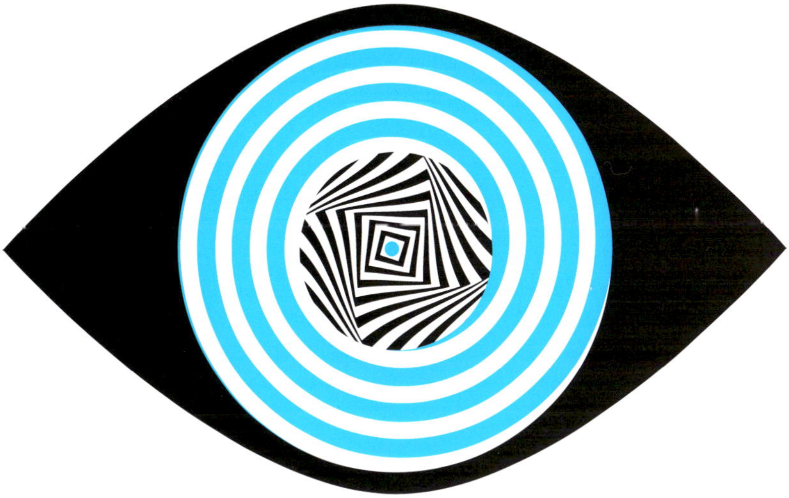

GIANNI A. SARCONE AND MARIE-JO WAEBER

Quarto Library

Quarto is the authority on a wide range of topics.
Quarto educates, entertains and enriches the lives of our readers—enthusiasts and lovers of hands-on living.
www.quartoknows.com

Concepts, text, and research: Gianni A. Sarcone

Design and Editorial: Tall Tree Ltd
Project Editor: Harriet Stone

This library edition published in 2019
by Quarto Library,
an imprint of The Quarto Group.
6 Orchard Road
Suite 100
Lake Forest, CA 92630
T: +1 949 380 7510
F: +1 949 380 7575
www.QuartoKnows.com

A CIP record for this book is available from the Library of Congress.

ISBN 978-0-71124-229-6
Manufactured in Dongguan, China TL012019
9 8 7 6 5 4 3 2 1

Words in **bold** are explained in the glossary on page 23.

MIX
Paper from responsible sources
FSC® C104723
FSC www.fsc.org

CONTENTS

IS SEEING BELIEVING?

Can you really believe what you see? This book will show you some amazing illusions that will trick your eyes and brain. It also contains simple experiments to show you how you can make your own incredible illusions.

How You See

At the front of your head are two forward-facing jelly balls, called your eyes. Rays of light are bent as they pass through the cornea and enter your eye through a tiny peephole, called the pupil. The lens bends the light rays a little more to focus them, before they pass through the middle of the eye and hit the **retina**, the lining at the back of each eyeball. As light hits the retina, it stimulates millions of light-sensitive cells, called **photoreceptors**. These send electrical nerve signals along the optic nerve to the back of the brain and a part called the visual cortex. This produces the final images that you see.

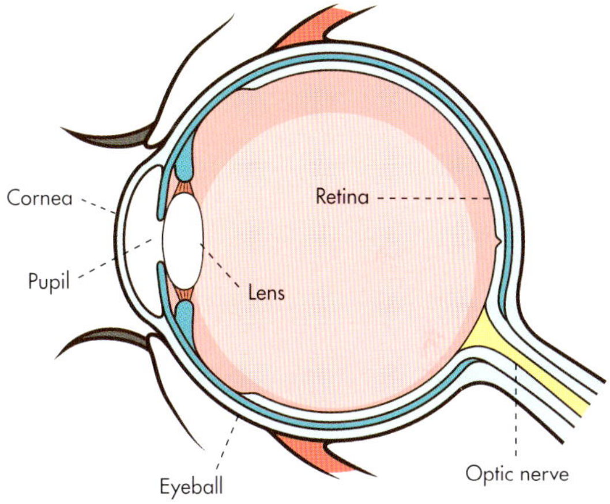

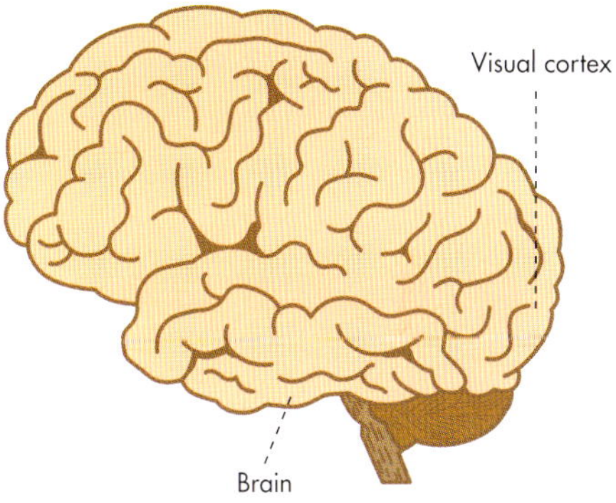

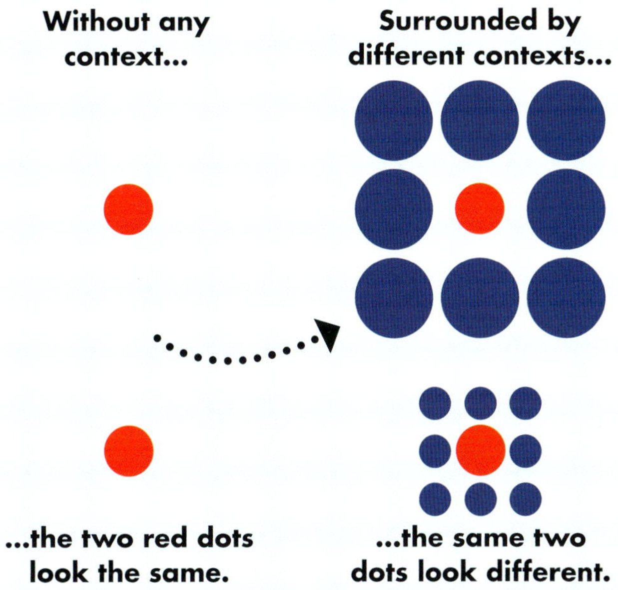

Context

While that all sounds nice and scientific, your seeing equipment can sometimes be fooled into seeing things that aren't there, or incorrectly seeing things that are there. These effects are called optical illusions. Many illusions are created because we don't see objects on their own. Instead, we see them in context and surrounded by other objects which can influence how we see things.

LIGHT

A tiny ant and a giant planet have something in common: they both cast a shadow! Light travels in straight lines, so if its path is blocked by an object, this creates a dark area, or shadow, behind the object.

Your eyes and brain use contrasts between light and shade to define the shape of objects. Your ability to see in three dimensions depends upon how light and shadow are laid out. When you see a surface that has two differently lit areas, your visual system enhances the contrast to see it more clearly. This is called "**lateral inhibition**," and it works so well that it can create a lot of powerful visual illusions!

Look closely at these four grids. Can you see gray blobs appear where the lines cross over each other?

A

B

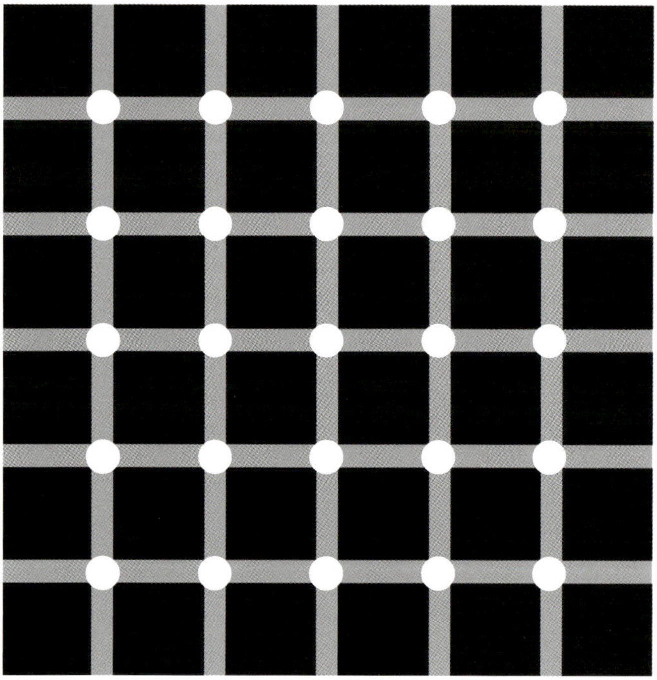

Scintillating Grids

You will find that the gray blobs are very faint in grid D and almost nonexistent in grid A. They appear in grid B, but the effect is strongest in grid C.

what's going on?

These mysterious blobs only appear when the crossing lines are straight, vertical, and horizontal. When this happens the contrast between the lines and the black spaces creates a lateral inhibition effect. This occurs when signals from photoreceptors in your eyes conflict with each other, creating the impression of dark blobs where the pale lines cross.

C

D

Playing with **Contrast**

Look at this cube and its reflection. Which one has darker panels?

In reality, the square panels of both boxes are identical and have exactly the same shade!

what's going on?

This optical effect is called "simultaneous brightness contrast." A color always seems brighter when surrounded by dark colors, or darker when placed on a light background. So the darker background in the reflection makes that cube appear lighter than the cube on the left, which is sitting against a lighter background.

An **Extraordinary Sofa**

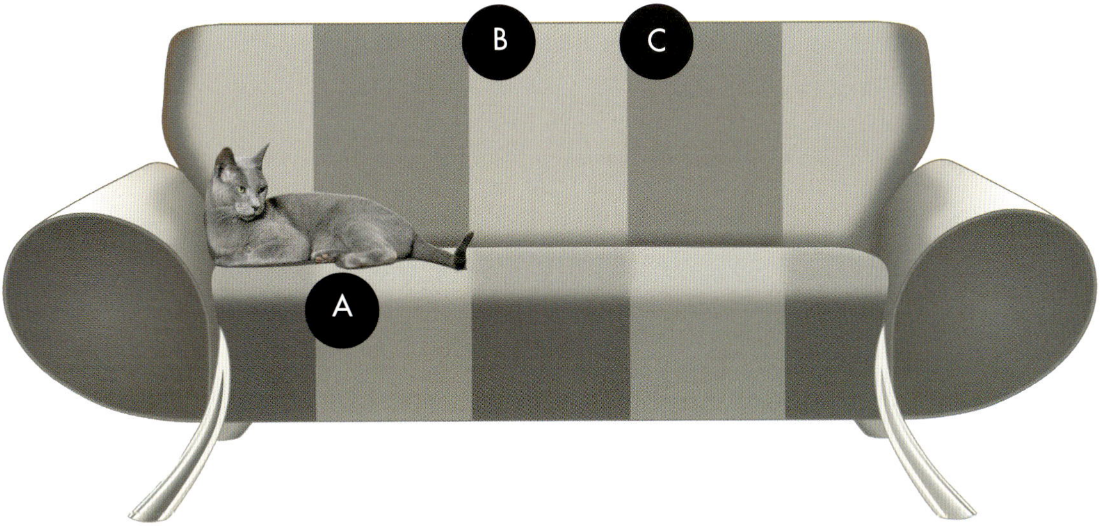

Which stripe on the sofa, B or C, has exactly the same gray shade as stripe A?

To check it for yourself, trace the template on page 22, cut out the holes indicated, and place it over the sofa so you can see which stripe has the same shade as A.

Stripes A and C are exactly the same shade.

what's going on?

As with the illusion on page 6, this effect is caused by simultaneous brightness contrast, where neighboring shades affect the apparent brightness of the colors next to them.

Dark Spot, Bright Spot

When you move a gray disk over a background with a changing shade, it will look darker or brighter, depending on its position!

WHAT YOU NEED

- Computer
- Free vector drawing software, such as Inkscape or Vectr
- Printer and paper
- Pair of scissors

1 Using your vector drawing software, draw a large rectangle with a linear gray gradient, which runs from solid black to white. Also draw a light gray disk. Print and cut these out.

Ask an adult before you download software from the internet.

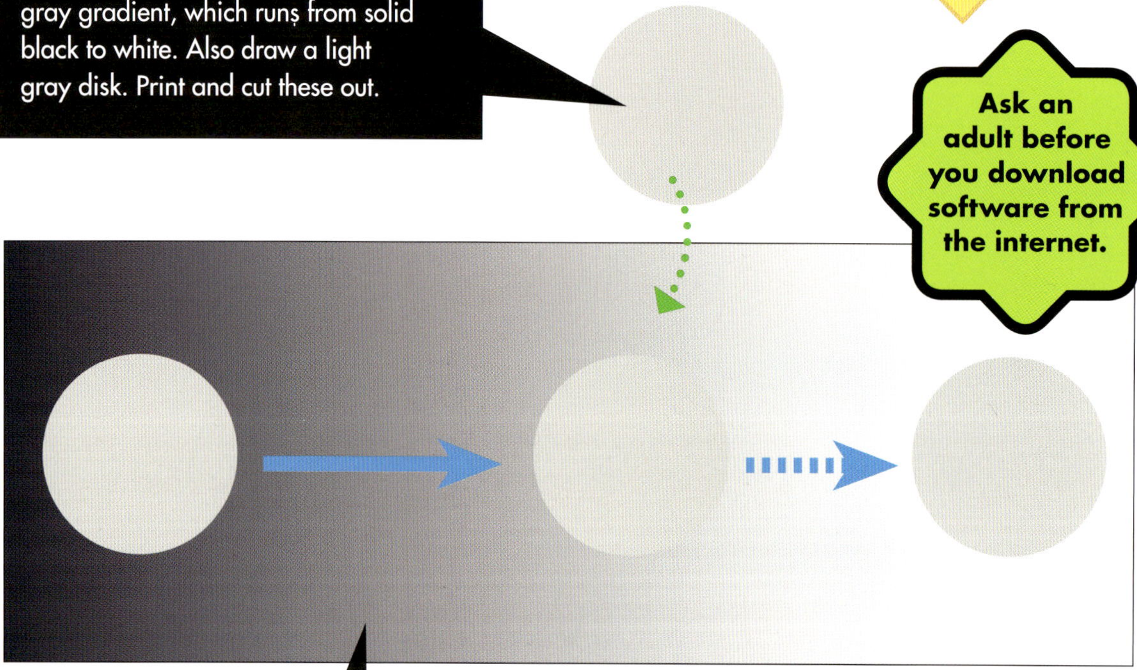

2 Now, place the gray disk onto the linear gradient, and move it slowly from the black end to the white, as shown above. You'll see that the disk appears to get darker as it moves toward the paler background.

what's going on?

This is another example of "simultaneous brightness contrast." It is related to "lateral inhibition," an effect that enhances the contrast of the outline of an object compared to its background. You can see examples of this on pages 4–5. It is called "lateral inhibition" because each photoreceptor in our eyes tends to inhibit the response of the ones next to it.

Puzzling **Colors**

Colors are not as definite as you might think. The way red looks to you will not be the same as the way it looks to someone else.

Your brain can interpret colors in surprising ways. Because you never see colors on their own, the appearance of any color is affected by the colors surrounding it. Under certain conditions, colors that are identical may appear different, while colors that are different may look the same.

What colors are the pale bars in between the brightly colored stripes?

What happens to the pale bars when they are next to two different-colored lines?

Believe it or not, all the bars on the different striped backgrounds are the same gray color shown in the top pattern.

what's going on?

This experiment shows the effect of "**color assimilation**" (see page 16). For example, the gray bars that are next to the blue lines take on a similar tone, and turn bluish. But when the gray bars are next to two different-colored lines at the same time (as shown by the far column of bars), they look like they have two tones merging into each other.

Color **Adaptation**

What color are this cat's eyes?

Check your answer by turning to page 22.

what's going on?

The eye on the right appears colored because of the purple surrounding it. If you look at the same picture with the purple removed (as on page 22), you can clearly see the gray eye. Thanks to a process called color adaptation, the purple **desensitizes** the brain to that part of the image. This subtracts a bit of purple from the gray eye, making it appear green.

Restoring **Color**

Can you make these faded gray parrots look bright and colorful again?

Stare at the bright dot in the striped square below the photo for about 30 seconds. Now look back to the photo and see what happens.

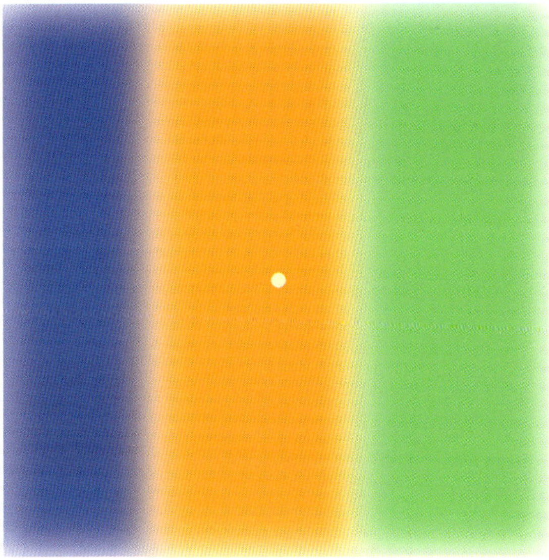

When you look back at the photo, the parrots' colors will have returned.

what's going on?

This effect is caused by color adaptation (see page 10) and it happens when your eyes take a few seconds to adapt to a light source. As you stare at the striped square, your eyes become desensitized to those colors. So, when you look back at the parrots, they will appear to have **complementary colors** for a few seconds! For example, the blue color creates a complementary orange **afterimage**.

Stained Glass Illusion

Take a look at the panes indicated by white arrows. Are they the same color?

Trace the template from page 22 and place it over the stained glass windows to reveal the truth.

When you place your template over the image, you'll see that the two panes are actually the same color, even though one appears to be green and the other red!

what's going on?

This strange visual effect is known as "**color contrast**" and shows that the same color may look very different when it appears against different colored backgrounds. This happens because our brain increases the contrast of the outline of an object in relation to its background.

Photographing **Levitation**

This trick will make your friends believe that you can float in midair. All you need is a sponge, some water, and a well-positioned camera.

WHAT YOU NEED

- Water
- Sponge
- Camera

1

To capture the feat of levitation with a camera, first you need to make a dark patch on the ground. Take a wet sponge and dab it gently on the ground. Try to make a damp patch that matches the shadow of you standing. If the patch is too wet, it will look too dark and the illusion won't work, so let it dry a little.

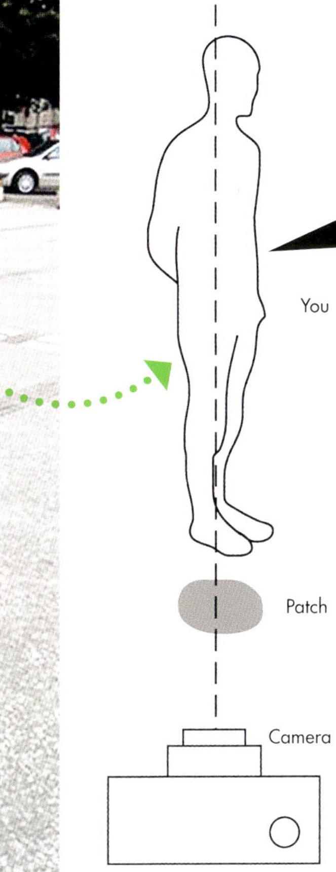

2

Now stand a short distance away (about 12–15 inches) from this damp patch and ask a friend to take a picture from the other side of the damp patch. To get the best effect, you must choose a location and weather conditions where your body doesn't cast a REAL shadow! You may need to move around the patch a little to get the best photo. Once your friend is happy with the effect, he or she can snap away while you are "levitating."

Rubber **Ducks**

What's happening to the yellow color inside these ducks?

Stand about six feet away and look at this picture before studying it close-up.

When you stand away from the picture, it looks like the color fills the duck outlines. But when you examine the ducks closely, you will notice that the yellow is only printed on a small rectangle.

what's going on?

Some colors, like yellow, have a low spatial **resolution**. This means it is difficult to see and define the borders of a yellow shape on a clear background. So, your brain tends to spread out low spatial resolution colors until they fill a dark outline, such as the duck drawings.

Magic **Heart**

Can you see an orange heart with a halo around it? Look at the picture from a good distance.

what's going on?

The apparent orange heart is created by the interaction of the black lines with the plain yellow background. The halo is formed where blue lines meet the small black squares. Strangely enough, if you really concentrate on the middle of the picture for a while (about 30 seconds) without blinking, you might even see the heart vanish completely!

Playing With **Assimilation**

Look at the letters T, I, and M in the first image. What colors are they?

The bottom image shows the same letters, with the colored lines removed.

It looks like each letter is shaded pink, blue, or yellow, but they are only made up of horizontal white lines!

what's going on?

This effect is caused by color assimilation. As with the illusion on page 9, our eyes mix the hues of the two colors around each letter, blending them to form a new shade. For instance, the red and green lines around the white "M" make it look yellow. Scientists are still unsure why this occurs.

Mapmaker **Illusion**

What colors are the land and sea shaded in these maps?

In the top map, the land areas between the orange lines look like they're shaded a pale orange and the sea areas between the blue lines are shaded blue, even though they are both actually white. In the bottom map, the colors and the apparent shaded areas have been reversed.

what's going on?

This illusion, called the "mapmaker color illusion," was used by early cartographers to help show one country from another. It is also known as the "spreading color" effect. People argue whether this illusion is due to a physical or a mental cause.

Neon **Colors Effect**

Stare at this electrical circuit for a few seconds and see what happens between the blue lines.

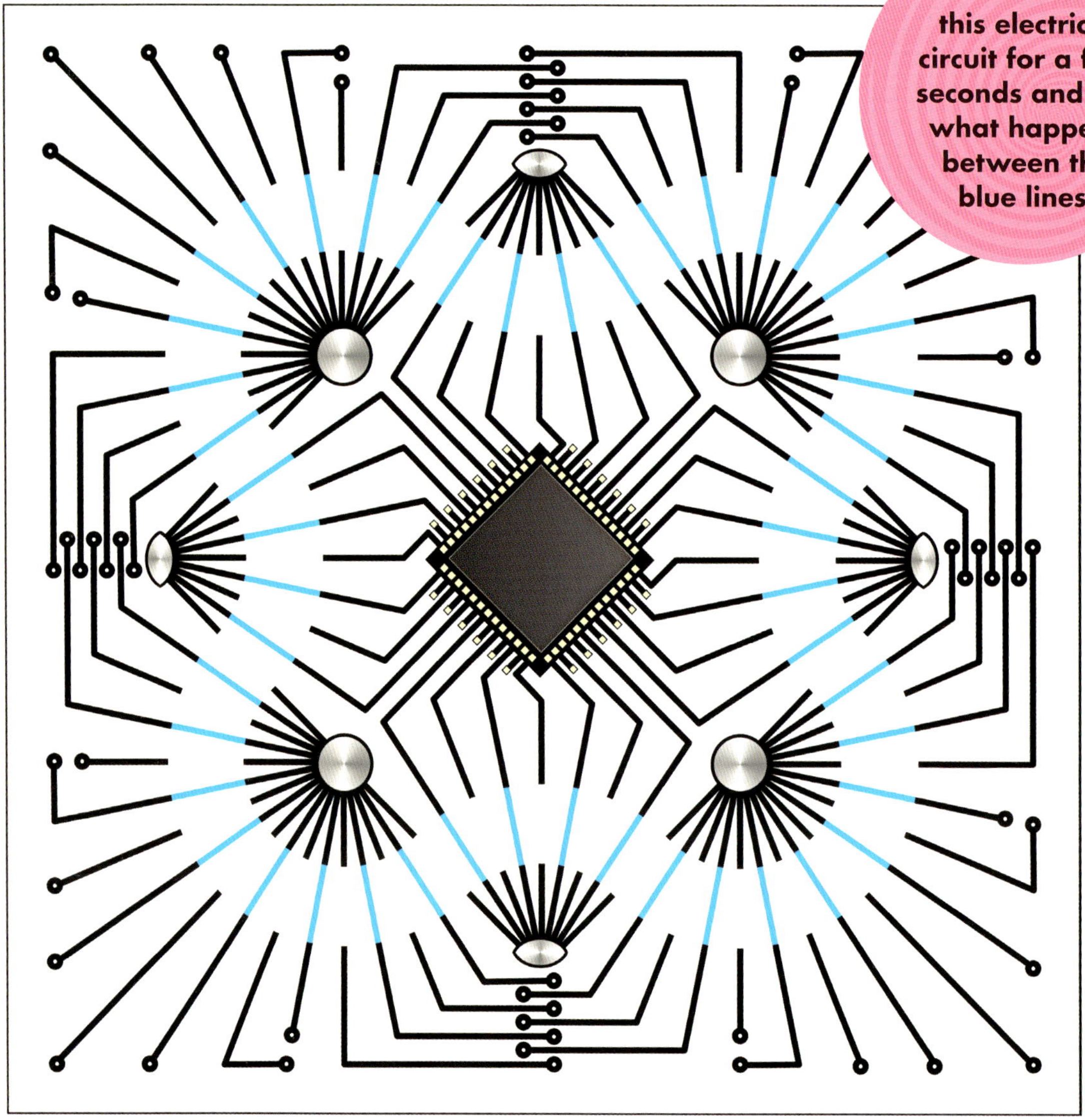

After a while, a bright blue twisting strip appears over the blue lines, even though there is no blue tint on the background (which is actually white!).

what's going on?

This shading effect is called "subjective transparency," "spreading neon color effect," or even "Tron effect." It was first observed by Italian researcher Dario Varin in 1971 and it may be left over from when our eyesight first evolved many millions of years ago in the dark depths of the ocean.

Making **Colors**

Is it possible to create a full-color image using just one color and black?

Image 1 shows a black-and-white image taken using a red filter, with another red Photoshop layer applied using "screen" blending mode.
Image 2 shows that same image sliced into narrow stripes. Image 3 shows a black-and-white image made using a green filter (it will still look gray). Image 4 shows what happens when you merge images 2 and 3.

You might expect to only see shades of pink. Instead, the resulting picture (image 4) appears colored even though it is only made with red and black lines. Even the Christmas tree looks a little greenish. What is even more surprising is that the decoration balls look gold. Amazing, isn't it?

Hole in the Hand Illusion

This simple illusion will give you the impression that you can see right through parts of your body!

WHAT YOU NEED

- A magazine or sheet of cardstock rolled into a tube and held in place with a rubber band

Hold the tube in your right hand up to your right eye like a telescope. Now hold your open left hand, with its palm toward you and its edge against the tube, in front of your open left eye. Focus both your eyes ahead and both images will merge into one. Slide your left hand along the tube until you see a hole in the center of your palm.

what's going on?

This effect is caused by binocular vision. Each of your eyes receives a different picture and your brain merges these together to create the hole in your hand.

Make Your **Own** **Hologram** Projector

Make your own 3-D hologram projector and amaze your friends by displaying a shining 3-D object that can be viewed from all sides.

WHAT YOU NEED

- Graph paper
- Pencil
- Pair of scissors
- Transparent CD case
- Craft knife
- Tape or superglue
- Smartphone

1

Sketch out a trapezoid shape on the graph paper, measuring ½ x 1½ x 2½ inches, as shown below. Then, cut it out to use as a template.

2

Ask an adult to use this template to cut four trapezoid shapes from a CD case with a craft knife. Tape or glue them together to create a flat-topped pyramid.

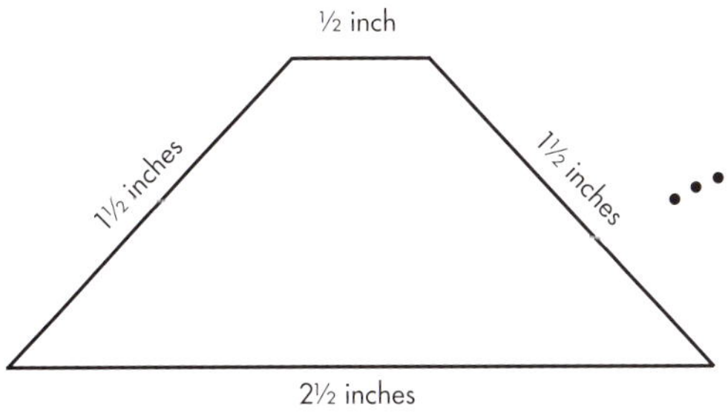

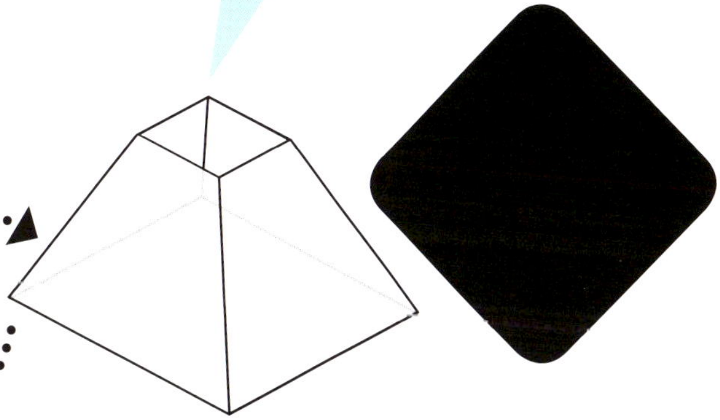

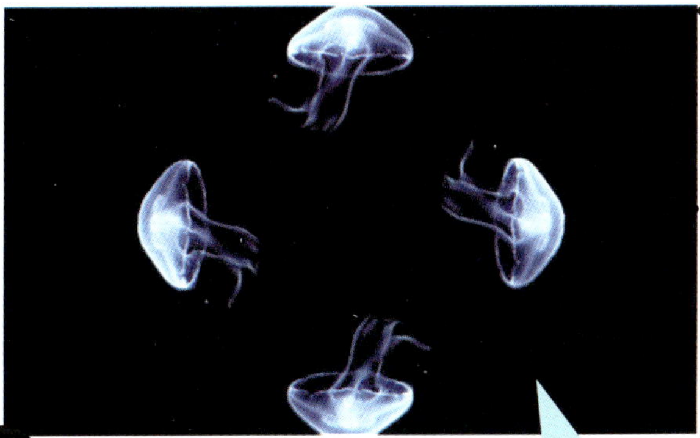

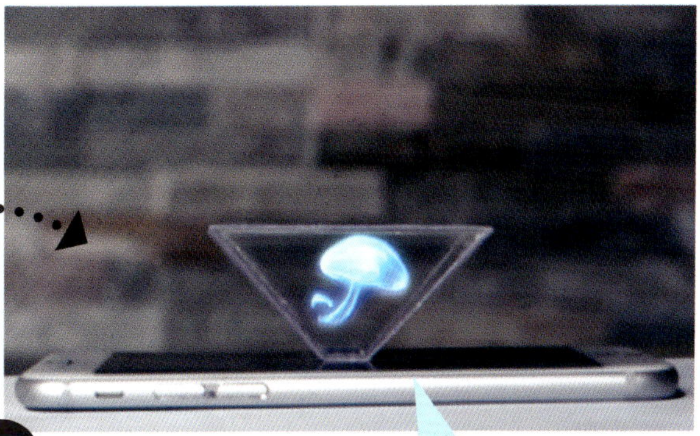

3

Using the web browser on your smartphone, search for "four-way holographic video" or "hologram video for pyramid" and choose the hologram you want to show.

4

With the video playing, place the plastic structure with the smaller base downward onto your phone screen to create a magic, mirrored, 3-D hologram that will amaze your friends!

ANSWER

This picture reveals the mystery of the illusion on page 10.

PAGE 10

TEMPLATES

Use these templates to check how some of the illusions work and to help you create your own.

PAGE 7

PAGE 12

GLOSSARY

afterimage
This occurs when you look at brightly colored images for a long period of time. The bright colors desensitize part of your retina at the back of the eye. When you look away or at a neutral surface, such as a white page, a ghostly version of the same image appears, but with different colors.

color assimilation
When the areas of color in a pattern are very small, the opposite effect to color contrast can occur and colors can appear to be more like a neighboring color. So a small or thin gray pattern may appear bluish when placed next to a blue background or yellowish against a yellow background.

color contrast
This is the apparent change in a color when it is seen against different colors. For example, colors may look more vibrant against a background that is a complementary color, or even paler against a dark background and darker against a light background.

complementary colors
These are colors that are directly opposite each other on a color wheel, such as red and green or blue and orange. When placed next to each other, these colors can create a vibrant optical effect.

desensitizes
Reduces the effect of something, such as a bright light or a particular color.

lateral inhibition
This occurs when a photoreceptor that has been stimulated by light stops or reduces the activity of photoreceptors surrounding it. Lateral inhibition enhances how well you see areas of contrast and, as a result, the edges of objects.

photoreceptors
Light-sensitive cells in the retinas at the backs of your eyes. They are triggered when rays of light fall on them and send signals to the brain, which turns these signals into the pictures you see.

resolution
How clearly an image can be seen. Printed images or pictures on a television or computer screen are made up of tiny dots, or pixels. The more dots, the greater the resolution, and the sharper the image appears.

retina
The thin layer at the back of the eye that covers nearly three-quarters of the inside of the eyeball. It contains millions of light-sensitive photoreceptors.

INDEX

PICTURE CREDITS

(t=top, b=bottom, l=left, r=right, c=center)

Dreamstime:
3t © Alexander Pokusay | Dreamstime.com, 3c © Suriya Siritam | Dreamstime.com

Shutterstock:
1 © Shutterstock/casejustin

All other images courtesy of **Gianni A. Sarcone**.